Femispheres

Also by Anamaría Crowe Serrano

Dall'altra parte
The interpreter
Paso Doble

ANAMARÍA CROWE SERRANO

Femispheres

Shearsman Books
Exeter

Published in the United Kingdom in 2008 by
Shearsman Books Ltd
58 Velwell Road
Exeter EX4 4LD

www.shearsman.com

ISBN 978-1-907500-59-2

Acknowledgements:
Some of these poems have appeared previously, or will appear, in *Ars poetica, Carte allineate, Damn the Caesars, Default, Fire, Fulcrum, Jacket, Masthead, Offsets, Osiris, Pagine, Red Pagoda Press, Shadowtrain, Shearsman* and *Triskell*. My thanks to the editors.

Cover image: L'Attesa, by Paola Perugini, 2006.
Copyright © Paola Perugini; reproduced here by permission of the artist.

Contents

Femispheres

For my wonderful children, Rachael and Michael
(a mis hijos encantadores, Raquel y Miguel)

Fireside story wood

Rainwords dropping leafless whispers
on the bark of a Lithuanian tree
      felled forest histories
      silver-laced in the rough silence of a snapshot.

The way a trunk insinuates a tree, the oneness
of our eyes, a touch.
           Me here.
             You there
amongst symbols – a blade of grass, a fairy twig,
shuttered bark flung back.
My room peers into the forest and I am the invisible
roots at your feet.

Mulling this tree, it slowly finds its former fullness
and motion on my wall
the feathered thought that carries it beyond image.
A murmuring of its voices
returns through the naked wood:
      this scarred grain is not a picture
      it is the wounds of a living poem
beyond the shy
      hand
      that clicks unutterable words

Mid-morning meditation

Unable to concentrate on work
suffering an internal knot
over characters and plot – I leave the desk
and the mini mounds of sawdust
vigorously mounting under it.
Woodworm. There is woodworm everywhere.
The house is being slowly eaten alive.
Sometimes it moans. Just a quiet creak
not intending to disturb, accepting
maybe even glad to be so relished.

Unable to concentrate on work
I hang my hair out the open window
spill it all out on the terrace
to get tangled in a dying witch
hazel in a cracked pot.
An ant zigzags across the tiles
an ant without a colony. Unemployed.
An old church pew pulls away
from its joints. It, too, is cracking along the grain
for lack of pious buttocks and bony knees
lack of feet and elbows to scuff it ardently
whispering the worn mantras of the world.
The ant is lost, the pew misplaced.
There is no God.
Pots crack. Beams threaten to give
and kill me in my sleep.
Hazelnuts in groves are going to waste.
The grapes are not yet ripe.
This is the sum of life to date.
It is a blessed day.

All things new

The energy – I hadn't noticed the energy
of your birth
your red face squeezing itself
out of breath – vitality
leading to the incessant questioning
that is all you
sucking, sponge-like, everything
from the birth passage on –
the ecstasy of discovery.
And now that you are gone,
this child's awe behind me
on a flight to Rome, squealing
with delight, rapture at every
movement of the plane
makes me want to cry
        at unexpected joy.

Green moments

the green moments of the day
have a sixth sense –
a distant space that quietly embraces
grassy ground, clinging
without thinking.
Wood lice and earwigs find a softness
in its stones that makes them
light, so light you could lift them
and watch fear
scurry to the confused corners of the
earth. Or you can simply watch
knowing life is quaking
within the crevices and in the rock pools,
deep down
where we are deaf
and dumb...

Largo

These tapping
metal-warbling sounds
come clinking
out of their outdoor case.
On a happier day they could be
birds in hands – brief moments
of simple pleasure –
shared feathers flocking...

A touch of untranslatable
about the way the here and now
unlocks their after-spirit
of grief like fits of hailstones
pelting fruit now absent
on this frozen tongue,
looking to drown a thought
in the dregs of winter sunlight,
trying to repair old strings
that have been pulled too tight.

for "Mr. Foo"

The expressions of old men have dug themselves
in the quarry of your wrinkled face
folding into and out of itself like water
washing centuries of sleep off sculpted stone
these hours of your first week.
They have carved the pleasures and pains
of all the lives that went into your making
until the moment you became a thought
drafted in darkness
and they plied their craft on you.

The multiplicity of your face
is proof that you will learn what you already know
everything they taught you
as time grows from days to weeks to needs
of different kinds, and you sweat like them
to find expressions worthy of engraving
on future faces,
to find knowledge that is no different
from quality workmanship
or from your blind instinctive search now
for a nipple to suck.

Pitter patter
for Raquel

Your hand is defiant in mine
straining to be unleashed like insistent rain
and break the silence below –
imprint itself on muddy ground
you love to tread
while you place the whispers soft between us
among the ferns, sure-footed as
echoes
rustling in slow motion,
as you must
in your cavernous way,
for me to listen one last time
and watch you

before letting go

Words on acanthus leaves

words on acanthus leaves   a sentence
stretching across the dawn   letters in the long
days   scribbled on the wind
every time I look   drifting by   all from you –
no second fails to tick
since you left and the garden cracks
once again
out of its shell   memories you planted
last year   all those kisses
gone astray   aimlessly
pollinating other mouths   a cry
in the dark and it could be you calling
from the fragile casket of my dream in the middle of the night
or it could be outside   a waft of marjoram   or a cat
sometimes it is   but it gets harder to tell
which is which.

Translation

To write poetry
is to say the unsayable
take a leap of faith through the empty page and find
its faltering tongue, its blocked ear,
its lazy eye, everything that has no proper place
and embark on a journey with these random parts
nurse them, cajole them, fight with them if you must
until you are one step closer to saying their name.
Ultimately
in the best poetry
love them to life.

To read poetry
is to hear life called
by its many unpronounceable names
because the poet has loved enough to take
that leap of faith for us.

To translate poetry
is to learn the poet's name
relive her faith, her love, her fight on the page
unleash a tongue, unblock an ear, redirect a gaze
restore things to their rightful place, journey
on a barque to bridge all random parts
nurse them, cajole them, fight with them if you must
until you are one step closer to saying their name.
Ultimately
in the best translations
relive to rewrite.

Genghis Khan

Old Khan betrays himself
kneeling on petals
bowing to the earth
pruning pink and yellow roses
in the trodden soil of his son's heart.

His canny face is softening in this afternoon
to the rivulets of his past, wrinkles
scattered across the plains
laborious, bedevilled territory –
the hardest to conquer is his own rose bed.

Who would have thought his hand outstretched
unbridled gesture in the garden of death
would be mistaken for the upright warrior
galloping on his steed,
and his son would respond with his shield?

Love me, love me not

. . . and then memory comes again
the long finger of the mind gloved
in its stubborn rubbery way round a daily chore
– always the daily chore –
wary of its old unwanted self
flexing slowly to appear unintrusive.
Sometimes it succeeds.

The gap it left is
now thick with grimy arguments
remorse
silence. In the mire
a hankering desire to yield to this
cautious coming, grasp the compromising mood
let it buff up neglect, scrub, rub old wounded
songs
or a look that used to blow you kisses.

Ah, you could
            be ticking a different
tune in a different time. You could be that rascal mouse
in a hickory-dickory-love leaf,
growing plump in summer fields
scurrying among fat fun
dandelion clocks tossed into whirling
satisfaction, love me, love me not,
laughing, devil may care, as
            a clothes peg falls from your washed out smile
and the rumble of the bin lorry down the street distracts you
because you've forgotten to put out the rubbish
and as always,
            it's too late.

Sky rave
for B.K.

There it is again! Everywhere
the barking sunshine bursting
mad mid-day dog clouds
sprawled in a whopping heat wave
yap-yap across the sky
the sky raving
slowly roving
       everywhere

it's the weekend
and it's summer and the children are
chasing bumbleflies and butterbees
with the cut-smell grass giddy
on their trail...
grass everywhere
stuck to their spirits
and their soles.

Oh to sit in the sun, anywhere
and ponder every day like this
the fizz of useless fun
the frowned-on idleness of bird
and be

living pieces of the puzzle
the poet calls
philosophy.

Taking stock

Some poets manage this, it seems.
They unscrew a leg – or an arm –
and cast it beyond the shadow
of the pen, piping hot
imagination bubbling back
as words, flowing verse, epic, even.

I, on the other hand, pause,
waiting for inspiration to fall
from the sky – when all that falls are stocks
and shares through the roof of my curious matter –
I've never known how to invest
wisely in anything that counts – and
I am humbled instead by a total lack
of everything
and an abundance
of precisely what eludes me.

How do you write that a stiff breeze
is burning behind your back, that the sky
is blue and open to suggestion, that woodworm
is boring wisdom into the garden bench
and that the daffodils –
always in April, the daffodils – are yielding
like myself to too much sunlight,
too much pressure
and whatever else the day throws up?

And what genre would it be, anyway?

Floods of flames

floods of flames in your eyes
unspoken words
inhabiting miscarried ground between us
                         setting seas alight,
quivering on your lash
like the rattle of a snake about to strike

        sweet bites that would burn my skin
        like a desert night
        sweeter than the pecked-out hollowed carcasses of men
        who dreamt of finding gold

I heed your warning
and I hush
        leave them well in your eyes
where they belong

they will be the mirage
when there is no asylum but my own wilderness
and distance is longer than it takes to count
each grain of sand.

Kinship

for Paul Donnelly

standing at the cliff edge about to topple
gulls come shrieking to strip me for their nest
and when they have pecked my cheeks and ravaged my hair
I will be a morsel in their beak and home to their young
clinging to a rock with twigs from the tree you planted

Magritte's curtain
a poem in two acts – for Katia & Riccardo

We three soldiers
have come far.
We have come bound. To each other and
to the rest of you. To what we have just done
and what you will yet do. Incarcerated
in prisons of our own making
we keep going, laughing –
though we are wounded –
over moor and mountain
bearing the burdensome gifts of civility.
We are three, defecting
as you, yes *you*, might visit a museum
on a Saturday afternoon,
for a bit of respite.

Things are different on this road, though we must
stay alert – more so than before. Here,
the weapons are all of the mind.
Apple rain begins to fall and we wonder
if it is a new strain of gift, something stalling
death, stilling life for the benefit
of our gaze.
My foot, pouting through my boot
paces onward, comrades in tow. We crawl
for miles, weary roses, hungry rocks, unaware
that you are gazing
at a portrait of three soldiers for whom
the artist drew back the curtain
and invited us inside.

Caged

Ah, yes – the words of songs
float round the compound gracefully,
falling into pouncing paws.
There is meaty passion in this tearing,
ripping of what once was nourishing on my page.

I lie wakeful, wary of the feast –
knowing outside, the plain
is probably singing silently
as far as the eye can see.

Nature

My nose has always stood out
like a poker stoking a poem
in the fiery side of life, and thanks
to it, the rest of me begins to grow
warmer, into some specimen
of fat grub leaving its trail
through a farmer's prized patch –

a grub large enough to be satisfied
it has repeatedly outwitted the farmer
and can happily endure a lifetime
of ugliness and spittley curses damning all grubs –
happy, at the end of the orgiastic cabbage
trail, to be considered by the farmer
a nuisance to be reckoned with!

A leaf

for Michael

Your hand, the leaf
falling from a tree
in mine
And you wonder why
I would think it was worth
saving.
You smile and turn
simultaneously to hunger, grinning
through milk teeth
the leaf forgetting
my fingers
as your hand
forgets mine

She is
for Mark

That woman on the park bench –
She is every season of your youth
your fears
your hopes
every anguished crease on your mid-life brow.
Deep in your throat she is all the names
you have forgotten
and names you will regret.

She is your lost child.
The sea and the wind are her only memories.
She sings.
She is flesh and blood
possessed, dispossessed
the demons of ambition
and success
what you cherish
what you despise.
She is the straw that breaks the camel's back
the nutshell for all arguments
the point and its refutation.
She is the stranger, the bogey man
your saving grace.

She is comfort in your bed
panic in your sleep. She confirms the moon,
its drag and pull, the rise of storms, the hand
of giant love in fairytales.
She cries.
She says all things
and is unheard by most, inconsequential
even to herself.

She sits on the shoulders of the world
thinking of you
and she is mute.

Noise

Noise changes the meaning
of everything   a laurel leaf
against a sound drop of busy
street   is not   a laurel leaf
but something closer to
an engine   the temporary hooting
of a shade of green.

Omit the revving and the drone
and its veins become
essential   odorous
a lingering moment
in the day.
Honking turns leaves
into tone deaf tunes.

Before the storm

Moored in the middle of a meal
from Mexico to Rome all I can think of is
where will you go from here.
You've given me your hand to hold. A giggling

offshoot gripping mine between sun showers
and hail. You alone amongst the crowd are choreographing
the afternoon because you have that gift of spectacle.
You laugh at a couple of ominous clouds and

toss them from your path. In the old days, you say,
they thought rain was God's tears. Sorrow pouring
on his people. You have a marvellous story
for everything. A life raft and a paddle.

At the table now, you make jokes and plans
your slim body changing inside my green top –
a love in progress – even as we speak. It is impossible
to cut the cord completely. That's what it means

for me to be your mother. In the nurturing we become
each other. Even in death we will be remnants of each other.
You flick your hair with the air of an older child
though you still have milk teeth crowding playfully

in your mouth. I must restrain myself as you ease
gently, gracefully into the storm. I will laugh with you
as best I can, listen to your stories, live
their intensity. This is the test. I will never know if

it is enough. Only you will be able to tell if I was here

for you, or whether I was floating too far ahead
too cautious, or charmed, to be of any use
drowning in anticipation.

The wood

Full-fat tedium spreads on her rump,
the backs of her arms, her belly, bulging
like the curvature across the horizon.
Under the branches of an apple tree
she dreams of sleep to shut out the day. The day
and its dearth of words and ways
clothes flapping on the line, the sum
of her accomplishment. She is woman,
mother of the earth
ground to a cultural pulp. Applauded. Her mind
ever alert to cross-currents
and impossibility.

Bel kiss

(on reading poems by Belkis Cuza Malè)

The Cuban poet is right.
Every day the search for more
than the lot allotted
to us breaks our back
and our spirit. We may
find refuge in the attraction
between what we express
and what we repress,
but it is a refuge without words.
Sometimes dusk, a sleeping
child suffices. In any case,
the raw material is bound to hurt,
pulling, as it does – against.

No Prince may kiss you, Belkis
but I do. I kiss you from my northern
femisphere
ebbing with the lipful tide
my tongue reaching the words
on the tip of yours.

To the prisoner sleeping in stone
for Tiziana

From stone sleep you are assaulted
by the waking in your head   half-immersed
compressed   in thought   unpolished
sight of a life sentenced to delight
disturb   recall the prisoner in us all
prey to human hands
you arch in agony, the angel in the artist's eye
yielding to the imbalance of the world.

Because of you the scales of understanding tilt.
Whether you know it or want it
talk bursts through your blanched veins
to and fro through time's continuous flow
your sinews fuel the thankless pigments
of our imagination   your spine follows the curvature
of yearning in the heart   in the mind   Because of you
we make the leap   to live form
to be content   converge in trial and error
a truth of vision beyond the Babels and Big
Bangs   beyond beauty   to the pull that frees you
from your frozen sleep and lulls you gently
towards interpretation.

Peace

to poetry: all truths
as undercurrents of the river
flow with the tow of one
                              word
unheard
despite being uttered in and under algae
round the stalks of reeds
each drop that fills the sea and breath
that is the air
the humble squall of birds

despite migrating on the wings of banners
to a thousand ports of call

across the world all depths of song
to truth return
in a simple word
                              denied

to harmony: the double-edged sword
of all other words
ill-sounding lies
                    lies
                         lies

Crush

amidst all the woulds and would nots
a stomach churned in knots. To be the centre
of the hunt, the one sought-after: who would
not? One the tender stalk of asparagus in a wood
hiding by the dry bed of a river. To be plucked
and savoured and sit in a sated gut. The end
an end in itself.
                  One the tender child
on the far bank of childhood. She turns
coyly on a breath, a *clin d'oeil*
the kind that would easily spot asparagus,
a lingering smile that bids farewell to innocence
while holding everything close to her chest.
To be embraced, in the end, by the earth
that feeds the roots – a simple need, a practiced kiss
a stalk that stretches to the sky.

The blank page

It's no use writing
on a blank page—
There's no such thing.

Emptiness is always
a confused moment
mid-way between the need to erupt
and the need to be filled—

Words and acts relentlessly
looking back, looking forward,
urging poems in our veins
to make them pulsate on the page
like new lovers
in the ripe moments
before sleep.

0 Brattle Street

0 Brattle Street
exists. A café
so narrow
it is not worthy
of a name
just four tables
and their chairs
an aura
strong enough
to conjure
rich roast
rousing
men and women
in aromas
you cannot see
They sit, sip
chitchat
browse
the daily news
peruse
a hurried world
made milk-
chocolate brown
silence frothing
in the smooth
draught
a hint
of cinnamon
through a door
that never closes –
for it has not yet
been opened

given that
in theory
it is not there.

In Sabina

…cast adrift
by a faint rippling
of wings, the sudden birth
of bird-speak flutters
across dips and hills

I know a language lost to me
lies out there
clitoral as the orange
pomegranate flower
open

to the thrill of thunder
clattering
and the lightning
in my soul.

Outside Palazzo Farnese

The men of Caprarola sit
lined up on a wall like tin cans
at the shooting gallery. Delicately battered.
You look at them and you can tell
they've been sitting there, immutable
for sixty years at least. Whole lives
lived on that wall. First

it was all talk of football.
Then, for a while they digressed
to much talk of women – a fiery
interlude hitting like a shot of grappa
in the daily espresso.
From the wall, they chose a wife
sat more upright as she walked to church
or to market with her mother
hand-picked for qualities all pleasing
to the eye.
Evolution took care of the rest.

Like swallows, the men of Caprarola
returned to their wall to sit
in much the same formation
they have been sitting all along to talk
less of women now
more of football
and how much better
it all was
back then.

Keeping it light

The time came. Out of the blue.
You knew it before I did.
Even afterwards I had trouble
admitting it. The denial of grief being
beyond logic.

What troubled me was not your knowing
or his death. It was your fear
of hugging him and saying you loved him.
You put it down to melodrama
making an unnecessary fuss
something too final about it all.
It was knowing you might fall
to pieces. Weep as a grown man.

He taught you that
and must have paid in his own way.
In the end, he, too, was afraid.
Still, it was a gesture to remember
that joke he cracked as a final parting
wanting to shake your hand.

6:45 a.m.

Drawn to the dawn
a dog in heat
rubbing against the light
sucking nutrients from the soil
Drawn
like a firefly glowing
fairy-like and furious
filling a still night with stars
searching for completion.

Drawn to the moment
bubbling underground
gaining pace at the raucous rate
or ravens rasping
among pine and cypress trees
and the steady scratching of woodworm
in the eaves

Drawn to the dwindling shadows
creeping across the valley
towards the window frame
wooden shutters poised for flight
waiting for the dawn to break
through the tiled ledge
and penetrate the room
ease the scratchingraspingrubbingscraping
of crumpled sheets howling
on an empty bed.

Building blocks

Curtly drawn in by the eye
to the epicentre of fault – mine
the only way to counter tremors is to lavish
love, it seems, to build with sweat and tears
structures sturdier than the collective mind.
It requires some engineering
for which I am ill-equipped.

My mud child is collapsing
inching precariously away
from the bedrock. Poles and stakes
organic arms so carefully constructed
to counter quakes, giving in an instant, ripping
runnels through the landscape of the gut.
You and you and him and her
hurry to misshape his smile
huff and puff his spirit down, to build
none other than a house of stone.

Quincy Market, Boston

There is a clapping I cannot hear
out in the market place
fall leaves falling yellow auburn
between cobbles pumpkinned
on my palate spiked
by lovers speaking Spanish
in Starbucks, chipping thought
wearing it thin like an encroaching
crowd, stripping me
of the carpet of leaves in the Public
Garden I tried to save for you
to expropriate New England's copper
sunsets between the pages of a book
on bees –

I'll take them back to you, pressed
the sounds you did not hear
the sights you did not see.

Gladiator

for Geraldine

She is a child who knows
about the Colosseum. There were gladiators there
who fought against lions
with the same urgency she fights for adult ears to listen
to everything she has soaked up in her eight
years. They were pumped with self-awareness
the need to hone the air like a perfect poem
captivate the audience, survive through
proofs of strength
and self
in sweat. They went in, she says, and they said
Toro! Toro!
shaking her arms in the red room
summoning wild fictions from suburban reality.
I laugh with her mother.
The cape of learning flutters in a gentle breeze
she doesn't quite understand
stirring up forgotten sand, cementing friendship
circles of the past turned strangely present.

Quitting

It's like brimming rain clouds. They burst
in the end because they must.
At saturation point things spill over.
Like beasts the size of a thumb nail
croaking in the dark. Tree frogs
bursting silence with their trumpet whistling
for reasons out there deep in plantains and palms,
engrained in their invisibility. Come day
they leave off because they must.
Knowing when. Knowing
to stop.

She too would stop by choice. The discipline
of music in the trees is for the night
and she is not an owl. Or a frog. She
is a butterfly, feeding silently off colour
skies made ready to sail. To keep going
is to slaughter the blueness of a day.
Mutiny is in her cheeks, her smooth
pubescent skin waiting to erupt, bury alive

those parts of me that acquiesce. Parts
I should have cancelled, called to halt
but did not. Because I was not taught. How.
Or when. Or that on occasion, perseverance
is a fault that grows to habit.

Breadmaking

It's in the yeast. A little at least
in warm water. Currents
rising, falling, pushing
land mass apart. In the bready gurgle
of yeast a part of me wants to be released
into molecules of water, the self-indulgent
heart of a bowl with a fulsome purpose
akin to crusty colours
thick enough to chew. There are endless seas
and grassy plains, mountains of the geoscape
that slice the soul in half. Of a night
out there there is comfort
in the smell of dough and the warmth
of your breath rising.

Mid-afternoon

mid-afternoon
mid-life
mid-dream.
Exactly where it's at.

The tempo of clouds
like ice floes
drifting off the window frame.
A slow clearance
of winter stock
to be replaced with fresh
organic afternoons
sky sheets the colours
of coral seas.

A curious customer
stops on the window ledge
magpie beady eyes
poking in at mountains
of paper work, the stale grey
landscape of last year's
wasteland
and instantly flies away.

Beyond the west wall
the sun is sinking
faintly gold
into the fault-lines and rubble
of other people's lives
on the shaken side
of the world
curiosity no more daring here

than boredom
a clear sky.

Today
exactly nothing
has changed
exactly nothing
has stayed the same.

New Year's Day

Day ONE yawns.
Its cavernous throat fire-cracks open
midnight wide, deep, dark
unknown and unexpected as the turning point of pain
grown familiar, suddenly hinting at reprieve.
The sun has upended on the east
probably peach-pink in the early hours before waking
those same colours of yesterday's leave-taking
when my heart turned grey-blue karst
skidding along an empty strand
pulse flapping on gull wings, the silence matted
with the prospect of migration into a new year.

It draws the most reticent mind forward
the most determined, the most depressed
the way it unleashes all those bubbles
of bottled past onto the stillness of a wintery slate
auguring promise amidst the infinite banalities
of an otherwise ordinary day.

An old man

It's important
just now, regardless
of the sun dwindling
or distance frosting the glass
to remember
that man in the children's costume shop
the man who lost his voice
the use of his legs
even his hands
the frail man sitting
in the middle
of the shop floor
upstaged by spacemen
and supermen
smiling at a little boy
because the day is long
when you cannot move
or speak
and youth so charmingly brief
but more
because the old woman's hand
after years of tending
and serving
still lingers lovingly
playfully
on his cheek.

Witness
for Mary Verner

In death she has touched you
as she never dared in life
being discreet, respectful
of other people's space.
Only her feet betrayed her
a hint of frivolity, or was it
philosophy
in the dance hall. But here

the clinical details are laid bare
in numbered columns, copied
certified, pursuant to laws
that govern exactitude
unaware that the omission
of her physical attributes
might only heighten them
for someone like you

that you would wish to know
she was not an anonymous
entry in a foreign record, that
she had been all flesh and free
in a way you never imagined
living beyond convention
to the point of moving you
three years on on a routine day.

More than the coroner, who
may not have even seen her,
the priest gave witness by his hand
in some fleeting way. Noted
her youth, quick mind

and aspirations, the fact
of marriage without any
expectations, not knowing

that these formalities would
bring her throbbing back
to you, sensitive to the
emptiness in pleasantries
and platitudes, the sadness
of a life untold – equally, the joy.
And then, the fallacy:
final witness reserved for facts
told by servants of the State.

Long hair

The longing gets knotted
in my hair each morning.
If it could be tugged at
with a wide-toothed comb

A gentle pull and the tangle
snaps painlessly away
falling with my stockings
by the bath and then I scoop it up

my hand a careful compass
bringing the orphaned bits
together avoiding the yellow stains
round the bowl gathering pile

upon pile with large depilatory swooshes
on hands and knees
trying not to think of loss
clumsy fistfuls of hair

nipped far from follicles,
fallacies and folly
I dump in the trash
a half-hearted gesture, really,

blitz the lot with the toothpaste tube
empty toilet roll, scraps
of snot-stained tissue. The thing
is

I'm never done. There are always
loose longings escaping – long, dark

flecks tangled on the floor
and after all that show of care

I get up again – I get up
and leave them there.

As if . . .

as if it were
the memory
of slanted trees
through the window frame
racing down the hill
driving their roots
hard
into the ground
with the strain

the farmhouse shutters
clapping
snapping pictures
of the winners
beads of olives pouring down
their front
those gnarled trunks
throbbing in the heat

as if the window creaked
when you opened it
to catch the memory
of a landscape
I have never seen
and the room
drifted
across the darkened ledge

Renaissance

the aura fascinates you –
that someone could tell
your mood just by looking
at the air around you.
what colour is your aura
you want to know as if your life
depended on it. anything
unexplained to fuel
your endless hunger
for learning outside
of the steady logic of numbers
which are so easy for you
something more challenging
the invisible, untouchable
capable of infinite mutation
infinity itself being another
maddening form of magic.

these pictures in the gallery
have turned your aura
bright. it's evident in your
eyes when you see a fruit
or a flower in the hand of an unknown
child, imitate a posture and imagine
holding it for hours. you gleam
with the discovery of
imagination – something outside
the logic that wraps you so securely.
of the saints madonnas angels
you take away with you
the intensity of pigments mixed
to make their giant feet, the dirt

speckled on their toes at the level
of your nose, their soles
and then, mysterious and unforgettable
their halos, gold and nudging
the folds of your mind almost
convincing you there might be answers
elsewhere and unnumbered.

Face to face

See this face
the lips cracking into wrinkles
like the final flick of a dying fish
eyes wilting on the river bed
a dried up remembrance
of running water. They wish
to sleep, to remember nothing
more than foetal warmth.
The absence of consciousness.
Simple sensory life.
But the journey wends on
down a long-necked rut, a ridged
breast plate, a mirage, memorable
not for breasts but for the candid eyes
and hands that stopped here
for a bite and gave these caved-in
bags something they do not have
a shape, a rhythm.

I think sometimes it may have been
enough, that brief valley, a rejuvenating
shower, but the more it disappears
the less inclined I am to believe
I should be satisfied with that
alone. It's a tough call. Where
is the poetry beneath these silver
lines, the metaphors of middle-aged
thighs? I tilt towards
motherhood and the thick cream
under my skin and in my mind
spills out, emptying slowly. You'd
hardly know to look at me. Oh

sure, I can scoop it up and dribble it
into a glass and it tastes
much the same, but you can tell
as well as I do it's not the real thing.
The real thing is going to waste.

Who crosses the frontier

*On visiting 'New Frontiers', an exhibition of
art from the new EU Member States, at the
National Gallery of Ireland*

Old women
babies suckling
barefoot boys
that woman's aunt
laying a railway track
whose dead husband ploughed
the mottled field out back
and changed the colour
of hard labour
and the beautiful young girls
with the glorious buttocks
any nation would wage a war over
swaying in blue full-sail
proud flags
under the whimsical red bows
of their summer dresses
even they drag the baggage of occupation
through the night
leaving shadows on the ground
between sickle-moon and mind.

Tulips

for John

The tulips are splayed
letting go a posture that seemed
so pert
perfect
I would have said
some days ago.
They are stepping out of a pastel pose
a pink formality
that lent them classical airs
dinner party grace
and with age – just days –
burdened by beauty
they bow, relinquish
everything
to gravity
and sprawl through the startled
shadows in the hall
tango
from their tight-lipped centre
towards the wall
the stairs
the brush
of humans unaware
of the petalled voice
that only blooms
when broken

The day

has lost track of itself
in the hobble
because of its reservation.

You say

the landscape is starved
the wings of birds clipped
a sharp-edged paranoia
swoops for the kill

of growth and flight
those places I've sought out
through you
for a moment's peace
silence, solitude.

The only way

it works is once removed
from the world
I don't know how or why
what makes it any different
the narrowness, perhaps,
of the ledge
good for a nest
perhaps the sun, the wind
that gives a sense
of wings.

Not even a proper love poem – but a song of sorts

On reading Pablo Neruda

Maybe
if I had thought about it
or had the wherewithal
in nineteen eighty six

to write one measly love poem
– never mind twenty! –
it would overflow with vibrant faith
the enthusiasm of budding love

awakening of eyes on flesh for the first time
drawn across a freckled back
the spine and the surprise
of pectoral tension

an intake of breath
delicate calves, ankles, toes
marshmallow sweet
soft and melting lips

the whole carnal lot, mountains
of biteable buttocks
cosmic in my hands
and in my mouth

with all the possible similes
the fireworks and metaphors of love
lost in an intoxicating torrent
blinded by sight itself

and the senses and the lack
of sense

and youth
knowing nothing of these things

relishing them nonetheless
like nothing else
before
or after

maybe
it would have been an earth-shattering poem
– even just the one –
to be remembered by from then on

acclaimed world-wide
award-winning
it might have made me, set me up for life
and you would be queuing to pay

for my words
forking out sums
that warrant invitations to lectures, dinners
book-signings

words that would most certainly
never have been meant for you
instead of getting
this improbable song of sorts

more primal
slightly off-key, something the words
in all the languages
of the world

will never quite succeed in saying
and the way I like to write it when I can
with my tongue
in your ear

A beast

There's a plant out there
with brilliant orange berries
summer and autumn
fused and for the life of me
I couldn't tell you
what it is
but that it is the colour
of your heart, of that
I am certain, a substitute
for your gaping absence
and the lack of sense
in this paltry life lived
without your words and wisdom
and it sustains me
on these sunny days just about
provides a fragile focus for the mind
in constant labour
to lose itself
forget about the physical
wrenching of body
from body
that deep cut of the cord
mercilessly bloodless
as to be almost unnoticed
albeit essential
and thereafter a wanderer
in search of its soul
with a few berries for sustenance
flushing out the beast that slowly
eats the hours
the days
the years

In the Andes

I see
the landscape of the soul stripped bare
the mountain labour over faces in the rock that are all Inca
mocking the tourist bus
I see
the wind sprout arms to catch the children as they dream over
the edge of cliffs and stare at us, oblivious to the precipice
I hear
the stars, the language of catharsis pouring from the milky way
I hear
tambo – a resting place
waiki – brother
cancha – flat ground by the river
picchu – mountain
I hear
wonder in the eyes of a shepherd asking about the sea
I touch
a cord, raw nerves, the blocks of ice that are my feet
I touch
base and crumple exhausted from exertion, hoping to overdose
on sleep and oxygen
I taste
glaciers
the purity of our path winding its way for miles over so many
millennia it looks like it was easily done and might be done again
I taste
laughter by candlelight, coca leaves
I smell
the clay we're made of, the dust etched in our skin, tiny flowers
that endure sub-zero temperatures
the past, the present, the future
proof that anything is possible, that things must change

On water

To write on water
gives intonation a roll
and stress a white horse rush

the words jutting above the surface
could be mistaken
for a small wave
a mere suffix that could run
a ship aground

The wake whispers
across the flat-scape
mercurial
rippling out in echoes.
If you were to speak
what you hush
your voice would cut the water
with the purpose
of a porpoise fin, just out of reach
each syllable breaking through
the mist eventually
churning up a chop

And that's how it is
the storm you brew
without a single word
your battle with the beauty
and the horror of the world
everything irreconcilable
too vast for words
poured out in a single drop
– a tear –
that causes tidal waves
and wreaks havoc on my shore

Sadness

for Giovanna Tresalti Toesca

It's hard to say what sadness is –
a loneliness of sorts that makes
the body leaden, alien to itself

an emptiness so invasive it would
require microsurgery of the soul.
But how do you remove a hole?

And then it's years of memory
that come careering out of nowhere
suddenly screaming their significance
making you carry the burden of pretence
that says you're in one piece
when you're really an amputee

Words

Words
slip-slide
over the rocks

loosely weaving them
together with a tongue
as limp as algae

rotting in the sun
each thought
punctuating the otherwise

easy flow of speech
tripping it up
on discarded entrails

heads and tails
and fear and shame
so it lands

on all the jagged bits
between the image
and the stutterance

Horizon

the eye wanders
from landmass
to where the water meets the sky
cerulean neither beginning
nor ending in blue
a favourite line of flux
inching out instead
to dreams, desire –
demarcations gone
the past well and truly
beyond that point of no return

it's only a memory
of drunkenness
punctured veins
booze and blood omnipresent
hinting thunder here
blizzard there
the harder you've worked
to paint those lightning sheets
out   flat-line the baggage
the eye travelling light
along another tack

Jazz in July

on grey cobbles
grey pigeon wobbles to a jazz
hobble beat

neck low
sweeps across the street
sweet weed
sniff deep

so high those fully fledged feet
feather flap feather wide
flying fine
tripping to the sky
to the blow cheek trumpet beat
the sun clap mellow bellow
of the pig-tailed cello man
merry finger plucking jam
big jazz bang
man!
what a Copenhagen afternoon

Sunflowers

Fields stretch
their sunflower heads
spread blankets of seeds
over empty streets
medieval miles
from the rain

the rows wizened yellow
fading, dragging
reason to the ground
same old same old
sun dance day in
day out, eyes glazing
till the odd head
swivels, lops away
a minor continent of summer
disappearing

it's not a dream
it's the boys, lost
in a fortress of flowers
frog hunting heaven
saving those faces
from the scythe

one for me
one for you

At 93

He is sitting on the couch
waiting for us
spruced up

they've slicked back his hair
changed his pyjamas, folded a blanket
across his knees

slippers like bunny rabbits
on his feet, a flurry
of female ministrations discreetly
conducting the scene

No trace of the incontinence
last night or the night
before the retching

No defiant breath raging
against the chink of light
behind the door

No sign of the troublesome intruder

He has been told of our arrival
it has been shouted
in his ear. Whether he hears or not
he nods

He has been instructed to disguise
the facts
in a child-friendly smile
and he does, even with a hint

of pleasant surprise as we walk in
full of apprehension
for what we'll find

Imagine
the brink, an abyss
we're that close. The door
will close when we leave. And that will be
all there is to it.

Instead we breathe relief
He doesn't look too bad
for now

Quechua

if you listen
you hear the wind
blowing you down

you hear the milky way
spunking along the sky
and the night
takes a deep breath

as if about to explain
the exact reason
it's so close to the black hole
at the centre of love
but refuses to get sucked in

you hear the origin of thought
pick a path
through the unwritten word
in heaps of dung penned in
by stone walls
where a universe of hens and hogs
daintily dance round each other
at some angle other than
the orbit of logic
and you know you've heard
the truth

you hear
silence
the desolation of altitude
with its eloquent patterns
etched to extreme locution

running with its tongue ablaze
in the glaciers whispering
as they melt

Abuelito

he comes quietly
rustling the leaves
in darkness
whenever we choose
to listen

all the answers
to the questions we never
asked, whistling
through the trees
and the cracks in the shutters

almost within our grasp.
His books and notes
are all in place. For now.
They are what little
remains save for

the howl of a wolf
or the trellis twisted
into memory.
The house is full
of children chattering

in the emptiness
his wisdom
his wizardry
more vital and dazzling than ever
now it's gone

The Sea – II

Bullock Harbour

all massive bulk, marauding
in the bay after carp and lobster
it comes looming from the deep
what onlookers think behind the safety
of the harbour is a rock
a slab of granite fixed on the sea bed
shimmers at first
then floats up, an illusion
giving the water plasticity

the eyes are what surprise
as they come into focus still
several feet under the sea, rising
through the excitement. You know
it's there on the tip of your tongue
this creature you challenge to the surface
moved by the thought that it's real
with a life of its own, that its beauty
lies in the power to thrill, as irrepressible
as its need to kill

The Sea – III

Seafront, Dun Laoghaire

we sit exposed
nude rocks, pocked and wrinkled
with their curls of algae
modestly insinuating beauty
impervious to the pull of gravity
gull wings spread for flights
of fancy

far out, a white sailed topper
tops the waves
where water gushes over
the mind, pen poised
for flotsam as we float on the cusp
old debris from the deep
waiting for the carcass of an image
lost at sea, enough proof
of existence to merit
a decent burial, regurgitation
into words at least

Tiles

Stacked against the wall
chattering hundreds high
wide enough to turn their whispers
into rumour

ochred lichen, dusky grey
the shadows in between exclaim
and sigh, triggering
the threat of avalanche
the whitewashed ones a mottled
pun on snow

they prop each other up
stop the slipslide fugitives
with one collective grind
their sum being greater than its parts
whether curved or angular, earth
cooked too fast
or chipped just past its prime

they're all agreed the roof they made
was worthy of the rain, its tickle
trickling towards the gutter
of a hundred years ago
bringing on a giggling fit

an imperceptible shift
that mirrors the hills, irregularities
of the backbone
that promise permanence
even with the house in ruins

Divers

They dive
deep down
the ones who dare
with total trust in oxygen tanks
and the quality of care
that goes into nurturing
something as basic as a breath

They dive for what they find
bubbling between the fissures
of anonymity
grains of sand stirred by fish tails
long-flickered out of sight
shoals of tiny species
gliding en masse
to camouflage weakness –
all the lessons of the world
flowing in semi-darkness and flawless
not the slightest hint of triumph
at their success

They dive to feel the beat
of their own heart, compressed
the rush of knowing they've reached
home in an alien world
where the rules are unknown
therefore unbroken
and the old self is shed
drowning the madness overhead
renewed for a moment
before the air
runs out

www.ingramcontent.com/pod-product-compliance
Lightning Source LLC
Chambersburg PA
CBHW030047100426
42734CB00036B/575